THE SIN OF LAWLESSNESS
A LETHAL PRACTICE

Mark T. Barclay

All scripture references are quoted from the
King James Version of the Holy Bible
unless otherwise noted.

Second Edition
First Printing 1993

ISBN 0-944802-01-X

Write:
Mark Barclay Ministries
P.O. Box 588, Midland, MI 48640-0588

Cover Design:
Heart Art & Design
501 George Street, Midland, MI 48640

CONTENTS

Scripture

Dedication

Introduction

Chapter 1 — Excuses, Excuses 1

Chapter 2 — The Love of Most . . . Growing *Cold* 11

Chapter 3 — Wolves . . . in Sheep's Clothing 17

Chapter 4 — Spiritual Criminals 23

Chapter 5 — Spots, Wrinkles, Blemishes 31

Chapter 6 — Bible Antidotes 43

Chapter 7 — Taking Heed to Yourselves 53

Conclusion

Prayer of Salvation

HEBREWS 3:12-14

"Take heed, brethren, lest there be in any of you an evil heart of unbelief, in departing from the living God.

But exhort one another daily, while it is called To day; lest any of you be hardened through the deceitfulness of sin.

For we are made partakers of Christ, if we hold the beginning of our confidence stedfast unto the end . . ."

DEDICATION

I dedicate this book to all the tares, goats, and dissemblers who have assaulted my ministry throughout the years and who have caused me to search the Scriptures daily, to make full proof of my ministry in the Lord.

This knowledge has caused me to deal with people scripturally and also to help many other pastors in these perilous times.

". . . I hate the work of those who fall away; It shall not fasten its grip on me."
Psalm 101:3 (NAS)

INTRODUCTION

Jesus warned us that in the last days the sin of lawlessness would increase. He forewarned us about the results of this in the body of Christ and how it would affect people.

Lawlessness always challenges authority and ultimately is designed to hurt people. Because so many people rebel, gossip, tear up, sow discord, maim, and openly sin, many people's love grows cold.

I am in love with the Lord and His Church. I know the Lord has commissioned me and anointed me in this hour to help His people. I write this book under *His* direction and with *His* permission.

I pray it will convict those who are in lawlessness and warn those who could be future victims. I pray it will help your life and straighten your walk with Him.

I'm sure this book will cause me unusual persecution, for good people may misunderstand my motives or misinterpret my words, while troublemakers will move against it with lethal blows, knowing it exposes their sin.

Nonetheless, I care enough for God's people and am committed enough to the Lord Jesus to write this book of warning!

CHAPTER 1
EXCUSES, EXCUSES

"Wherefore lay apart all filthiness and superfluity of naughtiness, and receive with meekness the engrafted word, which is able to save your souls.

But be ye doers of the word, and not hearers only, deceiving your own selves."

James 1:21-22

I have found that much of the body of Christ today is suspicious and quite accusatory toward leadership and each other. It's so easy to point a finger and say, "It's *his* fault!"

In this first chapter, I've chosen some of the most famous quotations and excuses used by troubled people today.

"IT'S THE PASTOR'S FAULT!"

No, it is not! It's no more the pastor's fault than it is your mother's! If you're in trouble, it's *your* fault. Come on! Take responsibility for your own actions and behavior.

One day, coming home from a church staff meeting where I had just dealt with a problem person, I turned to Vickie and expressed my disappointment on the blame I received for dealing with this man. She said to me, "That's the way it goes. They sin, they are in violation, they break the rules, they gossip, etc. Then when you, as their pastor, deal with them, they put the blame on you."

Listen, friend, it's your mouth—put a guard on it. It's your heart—protect it. It's your mind—renew it. They're your feelings—mend them.

"HE DOESN'T HAVE A SHEPHERD'S HEART!"

I've heard this many times over the years. There are people who think they know all there is to know about everything. They themselves are not (and never have been) a pastor, but somehow they feel that they know what one is.

Most Christians think a good shepherd is the one who is soft and easy, soft spoken, never confronting, always politicking, and very cordial. They compare each of us pastors to a clergyman they once knew or a hireling they once supported.

Pastoring is not a popularity contest or a race to see who can collect the most the quickest. No, rather, it's an awesome appointment by the Head of the Church to be responsible for and to give an account of the final condition of the souls of men. Let's not forget the Chief Shepherd, the one who is called the Good Shepherd; you know—Jesus! Read Matthew, Mark, Luke, and John, and you'll be surprised at the Shepherd you find in there. He called religious rulers names (Matt. 23:33). He told them their disciples were hell bound (Matt. 23:15). He made a whip and turned over tables in the temple (John 2:15). He rebuked his helpers in front of others (Matt. 16:23). He confronted people about their sin (John 4:16-18). He observed people in the area of their money and offerings (Mark 12:41-42). He allowed people whom others judged as less than socially affluent to join his staff (Acts 4:13) . . . and many more startling facts! His name, once again, is Jesus!

According to a high percentage of Christian people, this Jesus would not be qualified to be a pastor today. Why? Because too many weak, prejudiced, soft, whimpering Christians would cry: He doesn't have a pastor's heart! He's too honest! He's too hard! He confronts too often!

"THE PASTOR HAS NO LOVE!"

What determines love? What is love? The Bible says that God is love. Love tells the truth. Love never fails. Love is unconditional. True love protects, warns, challenges, and provokes you to improve.

A seven-year-old boy was playing in his yard, had wandered off course some, and was sitting in the road. His father saw him and was concerned for his well-being. His dad was a sweet dad, a good man. He really loved his son. He noticed, in his concern, that a large truck was coming down the street and that it was going to maim or kill his son. He desperately ran to the door to warn his boy to get out of the street.

The man opened that door and softly, with a tender heart, tried to warn the boy. He spoke it again with even more tender love. It was soon too late; the truck had taken the boy's life. That father could have saved his son if he wouldn't have been afraid to raise his voice and shout out a lifesaving scream. True love disciplines, and it warns. It is honest and doesn't care if feelings are hurt or if words are misunderstood.

3

We need these *true love* preachers in our churches today, ones who love you enough to confront you. They love you enough to tell you the truth. They will give you what seems to be an impolite, harsh warning at the risk of hurting your feelings in order to save your soul. A good shepherd knows that hurt feelings can mend, but allowing you to get off course could be eternally fatal.

"IT'S A CULT!"

Nowadays, anything people don't understand is a cult. If it's new, it must be a cult. If it's different, it must be "cultish." If the pastor is at all authoritative, he must have a spirit of control. The truth is, most of the cults go unnoticed, while the works of God get persecuted.

I have found that most people who cry "Cult!" don't even know the definition of the word. Oh, and by the way, almost all of the preachers and religious people of that day considered Jesus and His followers a cult. After all, He spoke as one having authority, and His disciples were in submission to Him. I wonder what those same "cult callers" are saying today!

"IT'S SHEPHERDSHIP ERROR!"

A few years ago in South America, a man started a commune and had hundreds of followers. His name was James Jones. I remember watching the news report of the tragic end of his mission. It was reported that the guards held people at gunpoint while a Kool-Aid drink (containing poison) was handed out to the people.

This news spread rapidly throughout the United

States, and the name *James Jones* entered every house with a television set. The devil really spread the word, and people all over this country grew paranoid. As this fear grew, it uprooted faith and hope in many people. It also uprooted almost all the Bible authority that was left in our modern-day pulpit.

Everywhere you went you heard Christians talking about cultish leaders. Almost every Spirit-filled (especially nondenominational) pastor who exercised any kind of authority or boldness was nicknamed *James Jones*. People became so paranoid that they really thought ushers were carrying pistols. It was a standing slur, spoken often of non-Board-run churches, that one should "watch out for the Kool-Aid!" What a great time people had with this, and what joy the devil got out of cheering them on!

The truth is, some pastors did go overboard (some with their involvement in people's lives), but that doesn't mean that all did.

All true men of God—whether pastors, fathers, or husbands—walk with authority, speak the truth in love, can't be bought, operate in boldness, and want things decent and in order.

"THE SPIRIT OF CONTROL!"

Another slanderous, antileadership phrase that floated around was "the spirit of control." Many people began to discern this spirit on their pastors (so they thought). Again, every bold, authoritative pastor was soon labeled as having a controlling spirit. If a pastor confronted perversion, stopped strifers, or chased off church splitters, he was labeled as having a spirit of control.

I remember one man who left our church in the early '80s who cried out this same thing. He said, "You have a spirit of control! Authority has gone to your head. You are seducing people." He went on and on. When he was done, I told him, "If I have such a spirit of control, it surely must be a weak one, because in all the months you've attended the church here, it *never affected you*! You were never submitted, you never obeyed, and certainly, *never* were you cooperative!"

ERRONEOUS SAYINGS

These are things that felons cry out to draw sympathy from others, to make the good guy look bad. The criminal is a public enemy and a nuisance, but he cries about how he has been maltreated by the peace officers, and sure enough, some people side with him. (You know, the marshall is the bad guy, and the outlaw is the hero.) How perverse!

For years people who were in trouble with church leadership cried out these erroneous sayings. Here is a list of some of the most famous accusations from these poor, torn, paranoid people.

- "It's the pastor's fault."

- "The pastor has no love."

- "The church must be a cult."

- "It's shepherdship error."

- "Watch out for the Kool-Aid!"

- "He's too hard."

- "He's full of pride."

- "It's a one-man show."

- "You'll be brainwashed."

- "He doesn't have a pastor's heart."

- "He's nothing more than a James Jones."

- "There's a spirit of control there."

- "The ushers must carry pistols."

- "Once you join, you can never leave."

- "All they want is your money."

- "He plays mind games with you."

- "They lock the doors and won't let you out."

. . . and the list goes on.

BUT YE SAY . . .

"Why do thy disciples transgress the tradition of the elders? for they wash not their hands when they eat bread.

But he answered and said unto them, Why do ye also transgress the commandment of God by your tradition?

For God commanded, saying, Honour thy father and mother: and, He that curseth father or mother, let him die the death.

BUT YE SAY, Whosoever shall say to his father or his

mother, It is a gift, by whatsoever thou mightest be profited by me;

And honour not his father or his mother, he shall be free. Thus have ye made the commandment of God of none effect by your tradition."

Matthew 15:2-6

This is exactly what people do today. They know what God says, but they still say something different. BUT YE SAY: I believe differently than that! I've always seen it this way. I'm not convicted that way! I was raised to believe . . . I've never heard it that way before. The church I go to teaches . . ., etc.

God says it loud and clear in the Bible, "But ye say . . . !"

"I'M JUST CONCERNED FOR THE PEOPLE!"

I've heard this many times over the years, but it's always coming out of the mouths of those who are in revolt. They somehow convince themselves that they love others. They also think that if they make a loud enough noise or a big enough splash that someone will listen.

These same *lifesavers* will violate the Scriptures; yet they will speak as though they are righteous.

In 1 Timothy 4:2, Paul said that they speak lies in hypocrisy; having their conscience seared with a hot iron.

Let me tell you, friend, anybody who says they mean well but does bad is not to be followed. Of those who claim to love you—yet they dissemble—beware. In Proverbs 26:24-25 the scripture says:

"He that hateth dissembleth with his lips, and layeth up deceit within him;

When he speaketh fair, believe him not: for there are seven abominations in his heart."

Be wise to these strifers and talebearers. Do not be found with them!

"I have not sat with vain persons, neither will I go in with dissemblers.

I have hated the congregation of evildoers; and will not sit with the wicked.

I will wash mine hands in innocency: so will I compass thine altar, O LORD."

Psalm 26:4-6

CHAPTER 2
THE LOVE OF MOST . . .
GROWING *COLD*

"And because lawlessness is increased, most people's love will grow cold."

Matthew 24:12 (NAS)

"And because lawlessness will abound, the love of many will grow cold."

Matthew 24:12 (NKJ)

How is it that *most* (or *many*) people's love will grow cold? I'll tell you how. They will have their joy and hope stripped from them by watching people around them willfully sin.

That's right. When a brother or sister gets mad or hurt and leaves a church, they always cause trouble for everyone. It's the same as a divorce (everybody pays, nobody wins, and no one is ever really free from it).

When a preacher falls into temptation and commits sin, it discourages many people and even causes young Christians to stumble. Many will say: What's the use of my trying? If that *great* brother fell, how will *I* ever endure?

When a church splits or has a split off from it, many family members are divided over it. This takes away their joy, and soon their love grows cold. When believers see evildoers prospering, they fret. They know that they shouldn't because the Bible says not to, but they do anyway. When church members see strifers hurt their pastor or the church and there is no evident sign of godly judgment on them, it seems to confuse them.

A skilled talebearer can spread a tale around the city and start a rumor so great that when it's heard, it discourages members of the church, and their love grows cold. When lawlessness and iniquity increase, they have a tendency to wear you down, strip you of your joy, and kill your hope.

God is totally fed up with church splits, dissension, hypocrisy, lies, schemes, accusations against the brethren, gossip, talebearing, and the bearing of false witness.

I realize that the following verses are Old Testament, but surely they describe God's feelings about the stench in the Kingdom today. I hope we never get to the place where God actually says the following to us.

> *"I hate, I despise your feast days, and I will not smell in your solemn assemblies.*
>
> *Though ye offer me burnt offerings and your meat offerings, I will not accept them: neither will I regard the peace offerings of your fat beasts.*
>
> *Take thou away from me the noise of thy songs; for I will not hear the melody of thy viols."*
>
> Amos 5:21-23

TRAMPLING PASTURES AND MUDDYING WATERS

> *"'Is it too slight a thing for you that you should feed in the good pasture, that you must tread down with*

your feet the rest of your pastures? Or that you should drink of the clear waters, that you must foul the rest with your feet?

And as for My flock, they must eat what you tread down with your feet, and they must drink what you foul with your feet!'

Therefore, thus says the Lord GOD to them, 'Behold, I, even I, will judge between the fat sheep and the lean sheep.

Because you push with side and with shoulder, and thrust at all the weak with your horns, until you have scattered them abroad,

therefore, I will deliver My flock, and they will no longer be a prey; and I will judge between one sheep and another.'"

Ezekiel 34:18-22 (NAS)

We see this lawlessness practiced daily in almost every church in our nation. People will come in and feast on the things they enjoy about the church. They will "amen" the teaching for a season. They will get all they can from that church, and then as they go, they will trample down the rest with their feet so no one else can eat thereof. It never ceases to amaze me. Not only will these ramchargers leave the church, but they must ruin it for everyone else who attends there. They don't realize they are in trouble with God.

These same shallow, unrooted Christians will come into the church and drink from the water. They will enjoy the altar services and sing the songs, but sooner or later they pull out. When they do, something evil possesses them to muddy the water so no one else can drink from it with pleasure. According to the Bible, they are troubling themselves under God.

SPIRITUAL DIVORCE

The attitude of divorce is vicious. It's gotten in so many people, even Christians, that it is causing devastation to the body of Christ.

This attitude not only affects the husband/wife relationship but also relationships within the church. Many pastors recently have suffered the pain of divorce. We have had people tell us to our faces how they love us, support us, and will never leave us. These divorcers are cruel and vicious people. They tear up the flock, lie about the pastor, try to turn the rest of the family against us, take everything they can with them, maim your reputation as often as they can, and flaunt their new pastor.

These people are in trouble with God!

DEPARTING FROM THE FAITH

"Now the Spirit speaketh expressly, that in the latter times some shall depart from the faith, giving heed to seducing spirits, and doctrines of devils;

Speaking lies in hypocrisy; having their conscience seared with a hot iron."

1 Timothy 4:1-2

It's quite alarming to monitor the level and speed at which people today are being taken out of the race. Seduction and deception seem to be having a revival, and by the dozens, people are departing. The spirit of the world is in some of them, and others have hearts of bitterness caused by a simple hurt feeling.

When someone has submitted to demonic doctrines, they will no longer put up with sound doctrine. When someone has been seduced, they will no longer be comfortable around spiritual, holy people. When someone is speaking lies in hypocrisy, they fool themselves and are convinced by their own lies.

When someone's conscience is seared with a hot iron, they are no longer sensitive and will behave in ways they once were convicted against. They will do and say things that they once judged others for doing and saying.

NO FEAR OF GOD

When people lose their true fear of God, they lose their respect for Him and His established authorities. This is why lawlessness increases. One person watches another person sin, with no repercussions. It seems as though you can live how you want, say what you want, destroy what you want, and no one can do anything about it. It's been so long since we've witnessed an Ananias and Sapphira episode that we may be in contempt of God.

This misbehavior, without vengeance or obvious judgment, seems to cause people's love to grow cool. Disappointment rises and, before you know it, many people are disheartened and disillusioned. When they are like that, they don't fervently serve the Lord.

Watch out for this! Protect yourself.

CHAPTER 3
WOLVES . . . IN SHEEP'S CLOTHING

"Beware of false prophets, which come to you in sheep's clothing, but inwardly they are ravening wolves."

Matthew 7:15

"For I know this, that after my departing shall grievous wolves enter in among you, not sparing the flock."

Acts 20:29

It bothers me that so many of God's people have no discernment at all. I would think that a sheep would recognize and sniff out a wolf way before the shepherd would notice him; yet it doesn't seem to be that way in our churches today.

Many so-called pastors are only interested in drawing disciples after themselves. They don't seem to really care about the condition of people's lives or their final outcome. These leaders are mostly politicians who will say or do about anything to attract a crowd. They won't tell the truth, won't confront sin, won't ruffle any feathers, and will consistently preach and teach milk-toast sermons. They live in fear of people. Saul lived this way and died as one who had never been anointed with oil.

Jesus taught us in John 10 that a real shepherd does not run from wolves, danger, or trouble. He stays and protects the sheep.

HARBORING FUGITIVES

"For the time will come when they will not endure sound doctrine; but after their own lusts shall they heap to themselves teachers, having itching ears . . ."

2 Timothy 4:3

"But refuse profane and old wives' fables, and exercise thyself rather unto godliness."

1 Timothy 4:7

Many so-called ministers today are not God's men. They are religious men, men of the cloth, men of the "church," men of the board, hirelings, and professionals. They have little fear of God and therefore don't meditate much on Judgment Day. They have little comprehension of the accountability they have to God for the people they pastor. To many of these teachers, it's simply a vocation they chose—it's their job.

"Obey them that have the rule over you, and submit yourselves: for they watch for your souls, as they that must give account, that they may do it with joy, and not with grief: for that is unprofitable for you.

Pray for us: for we trust we have a good conscience, in all things willing to live honestly."

Hebrews 13:17-18

Many church leaders boast and pride themselves on the number of people who follow their teaching and come to their gatherings. The truth is, most churches that seem to be growing are not reaping the lost; they simply are collecting members from another's congregation. We are more into transfers today than converts. (Sometimes I feel like giving them a transit card, like the airlines do, so everyone will know they won't be residing here, they are just passing through.)

Every church has people coming and going. There are different reasons for this. Some are legitimate, some are ridiculous. It's almost a full-time job just keeping track of incoming people. However, it's a task that godly pastors must give themselves to.

How do you know, pastor, how a new person in your church left his last church? Maybe you are harboring a fugitive. Maybe this person who smiles just right, says all the right things to you, and gives a bunch was really a felon in the last church. Are you harboring a fugitive (one running from authority, hoping not to be exposed)?

I highly recommend that you do some homework on incoming people. Where are they coming from? Who was their last pastor? Are they in good standing in their past church? Will their last pastor give them an endorsement? Did they tear up the flock they left behind?

Listen, friend, even if you are good at this, you will miss some people if you pastor a fast-growing church. Even so, don't purposely harbor fugitives. No, I'm not saying we should turn people away from our church meetings— even troubled people can repent and do good. If you find out that people are from another church, then find out from them why they left and why they joined you. Call their previous pastor and get a damage report.

Once you've done this you can confront these new

members, teach them, and lead them to repentance. Then they can close their past with a good conscience and go on to serve the Lord.

Some of these people-hungry pastors will not only receive another man's trouble but will appoint them to office. What a violation of true Bible ethics.

One young man came to a city and expected to fit in and work with the other pastors there. Initially, the pastors received him at his word and even helped him financially to get the new church started. After a few weeks they noticed this young man was collecting and appointing to office all the troublemakers in the city. Listen, everybody knows that when you start a new church, this is who comes first. But a wise shepherd will not appoint these fugitives to office or put them on staff.

One of these pastors finally went to this young novice-of-a-shepherd and confronted him. "How do you expect us to work together when my congregation sees you appointing to office the very same people who have been marked for causing division among us?" "How can we do meetings together when you have as your key leaders the same people who purposely split our church?"

One young man joined our ministry, and soon after, railing accusations came from the city he had moved from. I confronted him privately. I called his last pastor. I talked with the people accusing him, and we offered to return to that city and make things right. This young man was willing to return to the church he'd left, stand in the pulpit, and ask for forgiveness for all he'd done to maim the work there. He showed true humility and repentance, and because of that, today he is in good standing with church leadership and is enjoying full-time ministry.

Four couples came to our church from another church a few miles away. As I noticed them attending regularly, I asked them why they were joining us. I then called their former pastor. He gave a bad report. I figured he would, but whether I agreed with him or not, it was important to their future that it be dealt with properly.

I let them stay in the congregation, but each week I sent a check to the pastor they had abandoned (it was their tithes that came through our offerings). I needed that money as much as anyone, but I knew better than to keep it. I did this until I could restore them and cause them to do what they could to fix their past. Today they are marching on with zeal and joy, knowing that they have no hidden sins.

Five couples left another church from another city and began to come to ours. I noticed them coming consistently, so I called their pastor. It wasn't a good report. I collected them all together in a classroom and welcomed them to our church. I advised them to say absolutely nothing about their past to any member of our congregation.

I taught them how I would deal with them if they spread strife and gossip in this church. I also taught them how to fix their past. I explained to them that they were welcome to attend the meetings here, but until they fixed the damage they had done to the best of their ability, they could hold no office and do no real work here.

I am not going to turn people out if they need help, but I'm not going to be naive either. I'm not going to harbor fugitives. I had a man on my elders team that needed to be relieved for a season so he could get his family in order. He started out great, but then his family became troubled. He was upset with me for setting him down.

A couple of months later he came to me and announced his departure. He told me that a pastor across town had offered him a position as an elder in his church. I couldn't stop this man from going, but I reminded him that it was God who made up the New Testament qualifications for leaders, and even if a pastor would appoint him to the office, God would still view him as biblically unqualified. How sad! What a mockery of justice!

Listen, believer, in these last days things will get tougher. You must settle down, grow roots, and endure. Stop running all around, avoiding your problems. Face your problems, confess your faults, prove yourself, and do good for God.

CHAPTER 4
SPIRITUAL CRIMINALS

"These things write I unto thee, hoping to come unto thee shortly:

But if I tarry long, that thou mayest know how thou oughtest to behave thyself in the house of God, which is the church of the living God, the pillar and ground of the truth."

1 Timothy 3:14-15

We all know that there are natural criminals who are a threat to peace and the well-being of the public, but is there really such a thing as a spiritual criminal? Are there really spiritual felons? How does God see all this?

In my years of ministry, and in my study of the Book, I have found it true. Yes, there are spiritual criminals who, to the church, are felons. They have committed crimes against the Bible, church leadership, and the brethren. They are armed and dangerous.

WHAT DID JESUS SAY?

"And fear not them which kill the body, but are not able to kill the soul: but rather fear him which is able to destroy both soul and body in hell."

Matthew 10:28

THE APOSTLE PAUL SAW THEM

"Let every soul be subject unto the higher powers. For there is no power but of God: the powers that be are ordained of God.

Whosoever therefore resisteth the power, resisteth the ordinance of God: and they that resist shall receive to themselves damnation.

For rulers are not a terror to good works, but to the evil. Wilt thou then not be afraid of the power? do that which is good, and thou shalt have praise of the same:

For he is the minister of God to thee for good. But if thou do that which is evil, be afraid; for he beareth not the sword in vain: for he is the minister of God, a revenger to execute wrath upon him that doeth evil."

Romans 13:1-4

Let me illustrate. We enter a grocery store in your city. There are two men standing there by a counter. One is behind the counter, and the other is in front of it. There is a cash register on the counter and both men want in it. One man is wearing an apron; he is the clerk, and he *has a right* to enter the cash register and deal with the money. The other man wears a bandana on his face; he is a robber and *has no right* to the money. He holds a weapon to the clerk's chest and demands that which he hasn't earned.

About this time, two men enter the door. They are clothed with uniforms and badges, and they carry weapons of peace. They are peace officers—police—and they see the men at the counter.

Guess who is happy to see them come in. The clerk is overjoyed that they have plenty of authority and that they will keep the peace. The criminal hates their presence, is threatened by the authority, and makes them his enemies.

Now let's apply this to church life. The only people who despise a pastor having authority are the church criminals. They are hiding something (a sin, gossip, their true intentions, etc.), and they fear that the pastor will catch them. If they can strip him of his authority, he'll be like a policeman without his gun. They can commit any sin or crime they want with no repercussions.

On the other hand, sweet, submitted, Bible-obeying saints are never threatened by a pastor who carries lots of authority. Quite the contrary. These good church citizens feel protected when the crimebusters are on the scene.

Another quick example: a driver speeds down the highway at 80 miles an hour in a 55-mile-an-hour zone. He is looking left and right for police officers. He has to beware of them because he is breaking the law. If he sees one, he will immediately adjust his speed to operate within legal limits. If he is pulled over and ticketed, he most likely will be upset with the officer for ruining his day and being unfair. He will expect the officer to overlook the crime and let him go, to speed on.

Another driver, cruising along at 55 miles an hour, smiles and waves at the officer who passes him, not threatened at all by the presence of authority he shares the road with.

Think about it, friend, the same principles apply to church life and God's Kingdom.

BENEDICT ARNOLDS

"For I know this, that after my departing shall grievous wolves enter in among you, not sparing the flock.

Also of your own selves shall men arise, speaking perverse things, to draw away disciples after them."

Acts 20:29-30

It continually amazes me how easily some people are fooled. They see someone rise up and go out in a bad spirit (speaking bad things) but follow them as though captivated by their boldness to deny authority.

There is a Bible principle here that will aid you. To rise up is the flesh and the devil; to be raised up is the Holy Spirit. To go out is the flesh and the devil; to be sent out is the Holy Spirit. Therefore, if *anyone* rises up and goes out, he or she is in the flesh or influenced by the devil. Don't follow them! If they are raised up and sent out, like in the Book of Acts, then they are motivated by the Holy Spirit.

If you have trouble believing that there are betrayers, read these scriptures and see what some of the greatest Bible leaders had to deal with. You will begin to realize that this action is just as prominent today.

THE BETRAYERS —

... OF MOSES:

Exodus 32

Aaron abandoned his integrity and sinned against God, allowing the people to sin. They all drank their portion of the melted calf.

Numbers 12:1-15

Miriam and Aaron grumbled against Moses out of jealous hearts. God judged them: Miriam with leprosy and Aaron with reproval. The whole movement of God was held up until Miriam was cleansed.

Numbers 16:1-11, 31

Korah gathered a following of 250 men and approached Moses in order to withstand him and his leadership. God judged them: The ground swallowed them up, along with Korah.

Numbers 14:36-38

The ten men who spied out the land caused the whole congregation to grumble. Those ten did not ever enter the Promised Land.

... OF JESUS:

John 6:66

His disciples went back and followed him no more.

John 18:2-3

Judas Iscariot, a close disciple.

Matthew 23:29-33

The religious rulers, pharisees, scribes.

Matthew 27:1-2

The priests, Jewish elders.

Matthew 2:7, 16

The secular government.

. . . OF PAUL:

1 Corinthians 5:1-5

Brother in incest – married his father's wife. The apostle turned him over to Satan.

1 Timothy 1:20

Hymenaeus – fell into heresy, tried to shipwreck other Christians' faith. Excommunicated by the apostle.

2 Timothy 1:15

Phygelus – an Asian partner who deserted Paul in latter years of his ministry.

Hermogenes – a traveling companion who deserted him in times of trial.

2 Timothy 2:17

Philetus – turned against the faith and the apostle and eventually denied the resurrection. Excommunicated by the apostle.

2 Timothy 4:10

Demas – a companion to Paul during his first Roman imprisonment, forsook the apostle and the ministry for the world.

2 Timothy 4:14

Alexander – a coppersmith who deliberately turned from Christianity and corrupted himself. The apostle said, "The Lord will repay him." Paul warned Timothy to watch out for him . . . dangerous.

Listen, friend, this book could not contain the thousands of names of those who have committed like crimes—who, for whatever reasons, have maimed pastors, have split churches, and have become carriers of life's worst plagues: strife and bitterness.

If it's you, repent. Cry out to God for the boldness to go back and fix what you've broken, seek forgiveness from those you've harmed, rescue those you've caused to stumble, and forgive yourself so you can go on in God.

There is nothing so comfortable as being in good standing with church leadership. God Himself requires and honors it.

CHAPTER 5
SPOTS, WRINKLES, BLEMISHES

"That he might present it to himself a glorious church, not having spot, or wrinkle, or any such thing; but that it should be holy and without blemish."

Ephesians 5:27

Regardless of all the emphasis today on the *no* rapture of the Church, the Bible tells us that Jesus is coming again. When He comes, He will be coming for the Church—the Church without spot, wrinkle, blemish, or any such thing.

For years we have thought those spots, wrinkles, and blemishes were merely flaws in our personality and character. We were of the opinion that God was going to purge us from these faults and shortcomings and that is what would make us a glorious Church.

The problem with this is that we didn't read all of our Bible, for it plainly reveals to us what these spots and blemishes are.

"The Lord knoweth how to deliver the godly out of temptations, and to reserve the unjust unto the day of judgment to be punished:

But chiefly them that walk after the flesh in the lust of

31

uncleanness, and despise government. Presumptuous are they, selfwilled, they are not afraid to speak evil of dignities.

Whereas angels, which are greater in power and might, bring not railing accusation against them before the Lord.

But these, as natural brute beasts, made to be taken and destroyed, speak evil of the things that they understand not; and shall utterly perish in their own corruption;

And shall receive the reward of unrighteousness, as they that count it pleasure to riot in the day time. Spots they are and blemishes, sporting themselves with their own deceivings while they feast with you;

Having eyes full of adultery, and that cannot cease from sin; beguiling unstable souls: an heart they have exercised with covetous practices; cursed children:

Which have forsaken the right way, and are gone astray, following the way of Balaam the son of Bosor, who loved the wages of unrighteousness;

But was rebuked for his iniquity: the dumb ass speaking with man's voice forbad the madness of the prophet.

These are wells without water, clouds that are carried with a tempest; to whom the mist of darkness is reserved for ever.

For when they speak great swelling words of vanity, they allure through the lusts of the flesh, through much wantonness, those that were clean escaped from them who live in error.

While they promise them liberty, they themselves are the servants of corruption: for of whom a man is overcome, of the same is he brought in bondage.

For if after they have escaped the pollutions of the world through the knowledge of the Lord and Saviour Jesus Christ, they are again entangled therein, and overcome, the latter end is worse with them than the beginning.

For it had been better for them not to have known the way of righteousness, than, after they have known it, to turn from the holy commandment delivered unto them.

But it is happened unto them according to the true proverb, The dog is turned to his own vomit again; and the sow that was washed to her wallowing in the mire."

2 Peter 2:9-22

"But these speak evil of those things which they know not: but what they know naturally, as brute beasts, in those things they corrupt themselves.

Woe unto them! for they have gone in the way of Cain, and ran greedily after the error of Balaam for reward, and perished in the gainsaying of Core.

These are spots in your feasts of charity, when they feast with you, feeding themselves without fear: clouds they are without water, carried about of winds; trees whose fruit withereth, without fruit, twice dead, plucked up by the roots;

Raging waves of the sea, foaming out their own shame; wandering stars, to whom is reserved the blackness of darkness for ever.

And Enoch also, the seventh from Adam, prophesied of these, saying, Behold, the Lord cometh with ten thousands of his saints,

To execute judgment upon all, and to convince all that are ungodly among them of all their ungodly deeds which they have ungodly committed, and of all their hard speeches which ungodly sinners have spoken against him.

These are murmurers, complainers, walking after their own lusts; and their mouth speaketh great swelling words, having men's persons in admiration because of advantage.

But, beloved, remember ye the words which were spoken before of the apostles of our Lord Jesus Christ;

How that they told you there should be mockers in the last time, who should walk after their own ungodly lusts."

Jude 10-18

This is why Paul wrote and asked the Thessalonian church to pray for him, that he would be delivered from unreasonable and wicked men (2 Thess. 3:1-2). Every pastor should ask his congregation to pray this prayer.

Now that we realize spots and blemishes are people, we should look a little deeper into the scriptures we quoted above. I've made a list below of what Peter described in 2 Peter 2:9-22 as blemishes and spots.

BLEMISHES

- Walk after the flesh

- Lust of uncleanness

- Despise government

- They are presumptuous

- Self-willed

- Not afraid to speak evil of dignities

- Speak evil of things they understand not

- They shall utterly perish in their own corruption

- Count it a pleasure to riot

- They riot in the day; everyone sees them

- Eyes full of adultery

- Cannot cease from sin

- Beguiling unstable souls

- Heart exercised with covetous practices

- They are cursed children

- Forsaken the right way

- Gone astray

- Love ways of unrighteousness

- Wells without water

- Clouds that are carried with tempest

- Mist of darkness reserved for them

- Speak great swelling words of vanity

- They allure through the lust of the flesh

- Much wantonness

- Live in error

- Promise others liberty

- Servants of corruption

- Better if they never knew way of righteousness

- They are dogs turned to their own vomit

SPOTS

- Speak evil of things which they know not

- Corrupt themselves

- Gone in the way of Cain

- Ran greedily for reward

- Perish in gainsaying

- Spots in your feasts

- They feast with you

- Feed themselves with no fear

- Clouds without water

- Trees whose fruit withers

- Without fruit

- Twice dead

- Plucked up by the roots

- Raging waves

- Foaming out of their own shame

- Wandering stars

- To whom is reserved blackness of darkness

- Murmurer

- Complainer

- Walking after their own lusts

- Speak great swelling words

- Having mcn's persons in admiration because of advantage

- Mockers in the last times

- They separate themselves

- Sensual

- Having not the Spirit

Wow! What an eye opener. We just made an awesome (almost fearful) list of wrong human behavior that is going to be purged away. I hope and pray that you don't fit any of these.

In looking at this list a little further, let's expound on some of these descriptions.

NATURAL BRUTE BEASTS

Both the Apostle Peter and Jude spoke of these brute beasts. Believe it or not, a couple of scriptures use the term "dogs."

DOGS

2 Peter 2:22

Dogs turned to their own vomit

Luke 16:21

Dogs came and licked sores

Philippians 3:2

Beware of dogs and evil workers

Revelation 22:15

For without, are dogs

EVIL BEASTS ... SLOW BELLIES

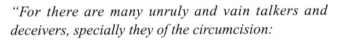

"For there are many unruly and vain talkers and deceivers, specially they of the circumcision:

Whose mouths must be stopped, who subvert whole houses, teaching things which they ought not, for filthy lucre's sake.

One of themselves, even a prophet of their own, said, The Cretians are always liars, evil beasts, slow bellies.

This witness is true. Wherefore rebuke them sharply, that they may be sound in the faith;

Not giving heed to Jewish fables, and commandments of men, that turn from the truth.

Unto the pure all things are pure: but unto them that are defiled and unbelieving is nothing pure; but even their mind and conscience is defiled.

They profess that they know God; but in works they deny him, being abominable, and disobedient, and unto every good work reprobate."

Titus 1:10-16

- Unruly

- Vain talkers

- Deceivers

- Mouths must be stopped

- Subvert whole houses

- Teaching things which they ought not

- For filthy lucre's sake

- Always liars

- Evil beasts

- Slow bellies

Stop reading this book for a moment and examine yourself. Do you have any of these beastly attributes? Are you acting like a dog? Are you speaking like a slow belly? Are you living like a spot? Are you a blemish to the body of Christ?

CLOUDS WITHOUT RAIN

These people are referred to, and compared with, clouds without rain, wells without water, clouds driven by the wind, unfruitful, trees whose fruit withers, twice dead.

This is probably the most blunt way one could describe a desert experience. We're talking about an awful dry spell. These people look like they are moist and filled with plenty, but they never produce an outpouring. Because of this, they have no real fruit. They are twice dead. They are doubly dead and plucked up by the roots.

CAROUSERS

"Being destined to receive [punishment as] the reward of [their] unrighteousness—suffering wrong as the hire for [their] wrongdoing. They count it a delight to revel in the daytime—living luxuriously and delicately. They are blots and blemishes, revelling in their deceptions (at love feasts) and carousing together [even] as they feast with you."

2 Peter 2:13 (Amplified)

"These are (elements of danger,) hidden reefs in your love feasts, where they boldly feast sumptuously—carousing together [in your midst]—without scruple providing for themselves [alone]. They are clouds without water, swept along by the winds, trees without fruit at the late autumn gathering time, twice (doubly) dead, [lifeless and] plucked up by the roots . . ."

Jude 12 (Amplified)

These spots are people who are bold as the lion and sneaky as the serpent. They will come right into your love feasts, feed themselves, and carouse together, looking like they belong, yet clique together as a band of wolves.

They are not ashamed to riot in the daytime. They sport themselves in their own deceivings while they feast with you. Jude says that they will do all of this without fear.

SPEAKERS OF EVIL

These people are sly with their mouths. They are experts at deception. Titus says that their mouths must be stopped because they subvert whole households. Peter warns us of their lack of fear to speak against dignities. He says that they speak evil of the things they don't understand. Jude says that they speak evil of the things they don't know about. Paul, in Acts 20, tells us to beware of these people rising up "speaking perverse things, to draw away disciples after them." Titus also called them, "unruly and vain talkers and deceivers" (Titus 1:10).

ABANDONERS

2 Peter 2:15

These spots are people who divorce and separate. Things don't go their way, so they pull out. They abandon. The Apostle Peter said that they have forsaken the right way and are gone astray.

Peter also told us in verse 19 that they were promising liberty to others, while they themselves were the servants of corruption. This reminds me of some people today who abandon their church, say they are free, and offer that liberty to others, and then we watch them flop around like a fish out of water. In 2 Peter 2:14 we read that they are "beguiling unstable souls."

WHAT WILL THE END BE?

"They profess that they know God; but in works they deny him, being abominable, and disobedient, and unto every good work reprobate."

Titus 1:16

2 Peter 2:12

They shall utterly perish in their own corruption.

2 Peter 2:13

And receive the reward of unrighteousness.

2 Peter 2:17

The mist of darkness is reserved for them.

2 Peter 2:20

Their end is worse than their beginning.

2 Peter 2:22

They are like sows, back to wallowing in the mire.

Jude 11

Perish in their gainsaying as rebellion of Korah.

Jude 13

The blackness of darkness is reserved for them.

CHAPTER 6
BIBLE ANTIDOTES

"Brethren, if any of you do err from the truth, and one convert him;

Let him know, that he which converteth the sinner from the error of his way shall save a soul from death, and shall hide a multitude of sins."

James 5:19-20

"But foolish and unlearned questions avoid, knowing that they do gender strifes.

And the servant of the Lord must not strive; but be gentle unto all men, apt to teach, patient;

In meekness instructing those that oppose themselves; if God peradventure will give them repentance to the acknowledging of the truth;

And that they may recover themselves out of the snare of the devil, who are taken captive by him at his will."

2 Timothy 2:23-26

Let me remind you that not all men have faith. In other words, just because somebody says that they are a Christian is no proof that they really are. According to Jesus, wheat and tares were planted by different sowers but in the same field. Though they grew together, their end results were significantly different.

Sheep and goats were all together in one place. They all expected salvation. They believed and spoke the same things, but their *doings* were different, and on *that* Day their destiny also was significantly different.

All ten virgins whom Jesus spoke of were together, and all had lamps and oil. Yet in the crucial hour, five of them were found wanting. Their end results were significantly different.

The Apostle Paul told us that Christ would present to Himself a Church not having spot, wrinkle, or blemish. I have shown you, in this book, who the spots, wrinkles, and blemishes are. Learn how to deal with them!

I've listed several scriptures below that will aid you in knowing Bible requirements for dealing with these treacherous people. My advice to you is that you study these and learn to walk in the Bible way. It's the only way God honors.

> *"Of these things put them in remembrance, charging them before the Lord that they strive not about words to no profit, but to the subverting of the hearers.*
>
> *Study to shew thyself approved unto God, a workman that needeth not to be ashamed, rightly dividing the word of truth.*
>
> *But shun profane and vain babblings: for they will increase unto more ungodliness.*
>
> *And their word will eat as doth a canker: of whom is Hymenaeus and Philetus . . ."*

2 Timothy 2:14-17

Acts 4:33 - 5:11

CHEATERS
Confront them.

Titus 1:1-14

UNRULY, VAIN TALKERS, GOSSIPS
Rebuke them sharply.

Titus 3:9-10

HERETICS
Admonish twice, then reject.

2 Timothy 2:23-36

OPPOSERS OF THEMSELVES
(hurts, attitudes, prejudices)
Don't strive, compete, or wrestle.

2 Timothy 3:1-5

SELF-CENTERED
Turn away.

2 Timothy 4:1-4

THOSE REFUSING SOUND DOCTRINE
Preach, correct, rebuke, reprove.

1 Timothy 1:19-20

BLASPHEMERS, BLACKMAILERS
Deliver over to Satan.

1 Timothy 4:1-6

THE SEDUCED AND DECEIVED
Remind them; warn them.

1 Timothy 5:11-15

YOUNGER WIDOWS—WANDERING
Marry them off.

1 Timothy 5:19-20

THOSE WHO ACCUSE ELDERS WRONGLY
Rebuke publicly.

1 Corinthians 5

INCEST/FORNICATION
Purge this one out.

Matthew 5:11-12

THOSE WHO REVILE YOU AND
PERSECUTE YOU
Revile not again.

Luke 17:3

THOSE WHO TRESPASS AGAINST YOU
Rebuke; forgive.

Acts 8:18-24

THOSE BUYING THEIR WAY IN
Rebuke; send to prayer.

Romans 16:17-18

THOSE CAUSING DIVISION
Mark them; avoid them.

SCRIPTURAL WARNINGS
TO PROTECT YOURSELF

Wouldn't it be great if we could trust everyone and take them at their word? It would be great to think that every Christian has your best interest in mind. I would love it if I could believe that no one wants me harmed. However, these things are to be taken seriously, and you must take Bible warnings to heart.

The thing that stands out the most to me is the heavy and consistent scriptural warning to us to be careful how we deal with these people.

> *"Brethren, if a man be overtaken in a fault, ye which are spiritual, restore such an one in the spirit of meekness; considering thyself, lest thou also be tempted."*
>
> Galatians 6:1

Notice the emphasis: *". . . considering thyself, lest thou also be tempted."*

> *"Having a form of godliness, but denying the power thereof: from such turn away."*
>
> 2 Timothy 3:5

Notice the emphasis: *". . . from such turn away."* *". . . avoid such men as these"* (NAS).

> *"But avoid foolish questions, and genealogies, and contentions, and strivings about the law; for they are unprofitable and vain.*
>
> *A man that is an heretick, after the first and second admonition reject . . ."*
>
> Titus 3:9-10

Notice the emphasis: *". . . after the first and second admonition reject; . . ."*

> *"I will set no wicked thing before mine eyes: I hate the work of them that turn aside; it shall not cleave to me."*
>
> Psalm 101:3

Notice the emphasis: *". . . I hate the work of them that fall away; it shall not fasten its grips on me"* (NAS).

"But the sons of Belial shall be all of them as thorns thrust away, because they cannot be taken with hands:

But the man that shall touch them must be fenced with iron and the staff of a spear; and they shall be utterly burned with fire in the same place."

2 Samuel 23:6-7

Notice the emphasis: *". . . the man who touches them Must be armed with iron and the shaft of a spear, And they shall be utterly burned with fire in their place"* (NKJ).

"Now as Jannes and Jambres withstood Moses, so do these also resist the truth: men of corrupt minds, reprobate concerning the faith."

2 Timothy 3:8

Realize they will resist their pastor.

"For there are many unruly and vain talkers and deceivers, specially they of the circumcision:

Whose mouths must be stopped, who subvert whole houses, teaching things which they ought not, for filthy lucre's sake."

Titus 1:10-11

Notice the emphasis: *". . . must be stopped, who subvert whole houses . . ."*

WHY SOME PEOPLE GET IN TROUBLE

They Are Troubled

Realize that some people do wrong things because their personal lives are filled with trouble (in their marriage, finances, health, children, job, or numerous other things).

When people can't cope with personal affairs, they normally can't cope with social affairs. This means they are going to do less than what is proper. It also means that they will blame the pastor, church, and maybe even God for the condition of their lives.

They Are Backslidden

"Backslidden" has the connotation of slowly moving backward in your Christian walk—to slowly pick up again the ways and thinking of the world. Most backsliders backslide while still going to church. They didn't seek the Lord relentlessly, so the care of other things entered in and choked out the Word and therefore strangled their lives.

Over a period of time they lost their zeal, joy, and desire for the things of God, and they reached to the world for consolation.

They Are Seduced or Deceived

Many people misbehave in the Kingdom because of outside influence. They begin to speak, act, and do things that are quite contrary to their normal convictions and character.

Usually these outside influences come by way of people or demons. People who are not close to God can be as destructive as demons—read your Bible.

People and demons can influence you through means of seduction and deception. When even a believer is seduced or deceived, he will do things, say things, and behave in an abnormal way.

Seduction is when you are influenced by an outside voice (a person or a demon) to do something you normally would never do, and you know (inside) when you do it that it is wrong. You are convicted about it while you are in the act, but the draw of seduction is so strong that you have trouble fleeing from it.

Deception is quite similar to seduction and arrives at the same results. Deception is when an outside voice (a person or a demon) influences you to do something you normally would never do, and while you do it, you don't realize it is wrong. You are convinced it is okay. You are tricked and fooled . . . you are deceived.

My pastoral experiences tell me that a deceived person is more treacherous to deal with than a seduced person. At least the seduced person is convicted that what they did was wrong.

THOSE WHO WILLFULLY SIN

Some people are just prodigals. They willfully sin. They pull together all their resources and go out on a fling. These people really are beside themselves after a while, and many of them wake up just like the prodigal son of the Bible.

After they party awhile and blow it all, they come running home, realizing that they've been living with, eating with, and smelling like the pigs.

OVERTAKEN IN A FAULT

There are some people who are totally ashamed of themselves. They are self-condemned for their wrong-doing. These are people who are overtaken in a fault. They became Christians, but they never followed through with the entire process. They never were completely convicted. Sure, they are born again, and they may have been water baptized. Many of them are even filled with the Holy Spirit, but they never really came away from the old way of living.

These are born-again church members, practicing Christian principles but still permitting worldly activities in their lives. Eventually, they are overwhelmed or overtaken by the fault and begin to give up on God.

THE WRONG FRIENDS

Many people just don't use the brains God gave them! They make commitments and relationships in the church, but they still have worldly friends. Some of them serve God faithfully, but they are surrounded by Christian tale-bearers, discorders, and hypocritical liars.

Eventually, these mockers will influence the good believer, and we will see him misbehaving and living wrong.

WHAT ABOUT YOUR FRIENDS?

"The righteous is more excellent than his neighbour: but the way of the wicked seduceth them."

Proverbs 12:26

1 Corinthians 15:33

Bad company corrupts good morals.

Proverbs 13:20

Fool's companion destroyed.

Proverbs 20:19

Don't associate with talebearers.

Exodus 23:2

Don't go the way of the crowd.

Psalm 1

Don't take ungodly counsel.

Don't stand with sinners.

Don't sit with scorners.

CHAPTER 7
TAKING HEED TO YOURSELVES

*". . . I hate the work of those who fall away; It shall
not fasten its grip on me."*

Psalm 101:3 (NAS)

*"Rescue me, O LORD from evil men; protect me from
men of violence,*

*who devise evil plans in their hearts and stir up war
every day.*

*They make their tongues as sharp as a serpent's; the
poison of vipers is on their lips. Selah"*

Psalm 140:1-3 (NIV)

It is your responsibility to guard yourself from people,
demons, and situations that will be harmful to you and your
Christian future. Many people don't seem to realize this.
They stumble through life as though there are no penalties
for wrongdoing. They speak as though there is no accountability for their words.

*"Seek good, and not evil, that ye may live: and so the
LORD, the God of hosts, shall be with you, as ye have
spoken.*

Hate the evil, and love the good, and establish judg-

> *ment in the gate: it may be that the LORD God of hosts*
> *will be gracious unto the remnant of Joseph."*
>
> Amos 5:14-15

The family of the prodigal son, in Luke 15, is a prime example for us today. Both the father and the brother of the prodigal *stayed* on the farm and kept the family going. The brother didn't even realize all that was happening; he stayed with his father and stuck to the stuff.

When the wasteful runaway came home, they were there to receive him. Did you ever think what would have happened if the brother would have left also and if the father, out of hurt and disappointment, quit?

This is for us today. You stay put, even if a brother goes to live with the pigs for a while.

How do we deal with wasteful runaways? You tell them the truth, receive them back when they come home repenting, rejoice for their willingness to be the lowest of all servants (yet still a brother), and help restore them as an active family member.

Read through the following scriptures and pay close attention to the things I have put in bold for you. They are warnings to us to live right and secrets of staying clean.

> *"Therefore **watch, and remember**, that by the space of three years **I ceased not to warn every one** night and day with tears.*
>
> *And now, brethren, I commend you to God, and to the word of his grace, which is able to build you up, and to give you an inheritance among all them which are sanctified."*
>
> Acts 20:31-32

*"But **watch thou in all things**, endure afflictions, **do the work** of an evangelist, make full proof of thy ministry."*

2 Timothy 4:5

*"But **continue thou in the things which thou hast learned** and hast been assured of, knowing of whom thou hast learned them."*

2 Timothy 3:14

*"**Holding faith, and a good conscience;** which some having put away, concerning faith have made shipwreck . . ."*

1 Timothy 1:19

"But in a great house there are not only vessels of gold and of silver, but also of wood and of earth; and some to honour, and some to dishonour.

***If a man therefore purge himself from these**, he shall be a vessel unto honour, sanctified, and meet for the master's use, and prepared unto every good work."*

2 Timothy 2:20-21

"This witness is true. Wherefore rebuke them sharply, that they may be sound in the faith;

***Not giving heed to** Jewish fables, and commandments of men, that turn from the truth."*

Titus 1:13-14

*"But ye, beloved, **building up yourselves** on your most holy faith, **praying in the Holy Ghost**,*

***Keep yourselves** in the love of God, looking for the mercy of our Lord Jesus Christ unto eternal life.*

And of some have compassion, making a difference:

55

And others save with fear, pulling them out of the fire; **hating even the garment spotted by the flesh**.

Now unto him that is able to keep you from falling, and to present you faultless before the presence of his glory with exceeding joy,

To the only wise God our Saviour, be glory and majesty, dominion and power, both now and ever. Amen."

Jude 20-25

"Wherefore, beloved, seeing that ye look for such things, be diligent that ye may be found of him in peace, **without spot**, *and* **blameless**.*"*

2 Peter 3:14

"Finally, brethren, pray for us, that the word of the Lord may have free course, and be glorified, even as it is with you:

And that we may be **delivered from unreasonable** *and* **wicked men**: *for all men have not faith.*

But the Lord is faithful, who shall stablish you, and keep you from evil."

2 Thessalonians 3:1-3

COMFORT ONE ANOTHER WITH THESE WORDS

"For the Lord himself shall descend from heaven with a shout, with the voice of the archangel, and with the trump of God: and the dead in Christ shall rise first:

Then we which are alive and remain shall be caught up together with them in the clouds, to meet the Lord in the air: and so shall we ever be with the Lord.

Wherefore comfort one another with these words."

1 Thessalonians 4:16-18

"Be patient therefore, brethren, unto the coming of the Lord. Behold, the husbandman waiteth for the precious fruit of the earth, and hath long patience for it, until he receive the early and latter rain.

Be ye also patient; stablish your hearts: for the coming of the Lord draweth nigh."

James 5:7-8

". . . Christ also loved the church, and gave himself for it;

That he might sanctify and cleanse it with the washing of water by the word,

That he might present it to himself a glorious church, not having spot, or wrinkle, or any such thing; but that it should be holy and without blemish."

Ephesians 5:25-27

CONCLUSION

Much could have been written here that wasn't. I certainly did not exhaust the subject of lawlessness. I could have given dozens of scriptures and illustrations in this book.

In conclusion, I thank you for reading this book all the way through. I ask you now to go back to the introduction and reread it. This will remind you of my motives for presenting the material to you in the manner I did.

I now pray for you, that you will put your foot down against sin, get mad at the devil, and do your very best to live right in Christ Jesus. I believe in you, and I agree with you right now, in Jesus' name, that you can do it.

Always remember that you will sin enough each day, not meaning to, that it will keep you repenting constantly. Practice nothing on purpose to crucify the Lord afresh in your life.

You are the righteousness of God in Christ Jesus—live like it!

PRAYER OF SALVATION

YOU CAN BE SAVED FROM ETERNAL DAMNATION and get God's help now in this life. All you have to do is humble your heart, believe in Christ's work at Calvary for you, and pray the prayer below.

"Dear Heavenly Father:

I know that I have sinned and fallen short of Your expectations of me. I have come to realize that I cannot run my own life. I do not want to continue the way I've been living, neither do I want to face an eternity of torment and damnation.

I know that the wages of sin is death, but I can be spared from this through the gift of the Lord Jesus Christ. I believe that He died for me, and I receive His provision now. I will not be ashamed of Him, and I will tell all my friends and family members that I have made this wonderful decision.

Dear Lord Jesus:

Come into my heart now and live in me and be my Savior, Master, and Lord. I will do my very best to chase after You and to learn Your ways by submitting to a pastor, reading my Bible, going to a church that preaches about **You**, and keeping sin out of my life.

I also ask You to give me the power to be healed from any sickness and disease and to deliver me from those things that have me bound.

I love You and thank You for having me, and I am eagerly looking forward to a long, beautiful relationship with You."

Other Books by Mark T. Barclay

Beware of Seducing Spirits

This is not a book on demonology. It is a book about people who are close to being in trouble with God because of demon activity or fleshly bad attitudes.

Building a Supernatural Church

A step-by-step guide to pioneering, organizing, and establishing a local church.

Charging the Year 2000

This book will alert you and bring your attention to the many snares and falsehoods with which Satan will try to deceive and seduce last-day believers.

Enduring Hardness

God has designed a program for His saints that will cause each one to be enlarged and victorious. This book will challenge your stability, steadfastness, courage, endurance, and determination and will motivate you to become a fighter.

How to Avoid Shipwreck

A book of preventive medicine, helping people stay strong and full of faith. You will be strengthened by this book as you learn how to anchor your soul.

How to Relate to Your Pastor

It is very important in these last days that God's people understand the office of pastor. As we put into practice these principles, the Church will grow in numbers and also increase its vision for the world.

How To Always Reap a Harvest

In this book Dr. Barclay explains the principles that make men successful and fruitful. It shows you how to live a better life and become far more productive and enjoy a full harvest.

Improving Your Performance

Every leader everywhere needs to read this book. It will help tremendously in the organization and unity of your ministry and working force.

Preachers of Righteousness

As you read this book, you will be both edified and challenged to not only do the work of the ministry but to do it with humility, honesty, and godliness.

Sheep, Goats, Wolves

A scriptural yet practical explanation of human behavior in our local churches and how church leaders and members can deal with each other.

The Sin of Familiarity

This book is a scriptural study on the most devastating sin in the body of Christ today. The truths in this book will make you aware of this excess familiarity and reveal to you some counter-attacks.

The Sin of Lawlessness

Lawlessness always challenges authority and ultimately is designed to hurt people. This book will convict those who are in lawlessness and warn those who could be future victims. It will help your life and straighten your walk with Him.

The Making of a Man of God

In this book you'll find some of the greatest, yet simplest, insights to becoming a man or woman of God and to launching your ministry with accuracy and credibility. The longevity of your ministry will be enhanced by the truths herein.

The Remnant

God has always had a people and will always have a people. Dr. Barclay speaks of the upcoming revival and how we can be those that are alive and remain when our master returns.